Short Voyages

Edited by Chris Buckton and Pie Corbett

CW00822724

Contents

OXFORD
UNIVERSITY PRESS

The Land Where One Never Dies

One day a young man said, "This tale about everybody having to die doesn't set too well with me. I will go in search of the land where one never dies."

He bid father, mother, uncles, and cousins goodbye and departed. For days and months he walked, asking everybody he met if they could direct him to the place where one never dies. But no one knew of any such place. One day he met an old man with a white beard down to his chest, pushing a wheelbarrow full of rocks. The boy asked him, "Could you direct me to that place where one never dies?"

"You don't want to die? Stick with me. Until I've finished carting away that entire mountain rock by rock, you shall not die."

"How long will it take you to level it?"

"One hundred years at least."

"And I'll have to die afterward?"

"I'm afraid so."

"No, this is no place for me. I will go to the place where one *never* dies."

He said goodbye to the old man and pushed onward. He walked for miles and came to a forest so vast that it seemed endless. There he saw an old man with a beard down to his navel pruning branches with a pruning hook.

The young man asked, "Could you kindly tell me of a place where one never dies?"

"Stick with me," replied the old man. "Until I've trimmed all the trees in this forest with my pruning hook, you shall not die."

"How long will that take?"

"Who knows? At least two hundred years."

"And afterward I'll still have to die?"

"Indeed you will. Isn't two hundred years enough for you?"

"No, this is no place for me. I'm seeking a place where one *never* dies."

They said goodbye, and the youth continued onward. A few months later he reached the seashore. There he saw an old man with a beard down to his knees watching a duck drink seawater.

"Could you kindly tell me of a place where one never dies?"

"If you're afraid to die, stick with me. See that duck? Until it has drunk the sea dry, there's no danger at all of your dying."

"How long will it take?"

"Roughly three hundred years."

"And afterward I'll have to die?"

"What else do you expect? How much longer would you even want to live?"

"No, no, no. Not even this place is for me. I must go where one *never* dies."

He resumed his journey. One evening he came to a magnificent palace. He knocked, and the door was opened by an old man with a beard all the way down to his feet. "What is it you look for, young man?"

"I'm looking for the place where one never dies."

"Good for you, you've found it! This is the place where one never dies. As long as you stay with me, you can bet your boots you won't die."

"At last, after all the miles I've trudged! This is just the place I was seeking! But are you sure I'm not imposing on you?"

"Absolutely. I'm delighted to have company."

So the youth moved into the palace with the old man and lived like a lord. The years went by so fast and so pleasantly that he lost all track of time.

Then one day he said to the old man, "There's no place on earth like here, but I really would like to pay my family a little visit and see how they're getting along."

"What family are you talking about? The last of your relatives died quite some time ago."

"I'd still like to go on a little journey, if only to revisit my birthplace and possibly run into the sons of my relatives' sons."

"If you're bent on going, follow my instructions. Go to the stable and get my white horse, which gallops like the wind. But once you're on him, never, never dismount for any reason whatever, or you will die on the spot."

"Don't worry, I'll stay in the saddle. You know how I hate the very idea of dying!"

He went to the stable, led out the white horse, got into the saddle, and was off like the wind. He passed the place where he had met the old man with the duck. There where the sea used to be was now a vast prairie.

On the edge of it was a little pile of bones, the bones of the old man. "Just look at that," said the youth. "I was wise not to tarry here, or I too would now be dead."

He moved on and came to what was once the vast forest where the old man had to prune every single tree with his pruning hook. Not one tree was left, and the ground was as bare as a desert. "How right I was not to stop here, or I too would now be long gone, like the old soul in the forest."

He passed the place where the huge mountain had stood, which an old man was to cart away rock by rock. Now the ground was as level as a billiard table.

"Nor would I have fared any better here!"

On and on he went, finally reaching his town, but it had changed so much he no longer recognized it. Not only was his house gone, but even the street it had stood on. He inquired about his relatives, but no one had ever heard his family name. That was the end of it. "I might as well go back at once," he decided.

He turned his horse around and started back, but was not halfway home before he met a carter with a cart full of old shoes and drawn by an ox.

"Sir," said the carter, "please be so kind as to dismount for a moment and help me dislodge this wheel sticking in the mud."

"I'm in a hurry and can't get out of the saddle," replied the youth.

"Please help me. I'm all by myself, as you can see, and night is coming on."

Moved to pity, the youth dismounted. He had only one foot on the ground and the other still in the stirrup, when the carter grabbed him by the arm and said: "I have you at last! Know who I am? Yes, I am Death! See all those old shoes in the cart? They're all the pairs you caused me to wear out running after you. Now you've fallen into my hands, from which no one ever escapes!"

So the poor young man had to die the same as everybody else.

Italo Calvino

A Table is a Table

I want to tell the story of an old man, of a man who has given up talking, who has a tired face, too tired for smiling and too tired for frowning. He lives in a small town, at the end of the street or near the crossroads. It's hardly worth while to describe him, so little distinguishes him from others. He wears a grey hat, grey trousers, a grey jacket and in winter his long grey overcoat, and he has a thin neck whose skin is dry and wrinkled; his white shirt collars are far too wide for him.

His room is up on the top floor of the house, maybe he was once married and had children, maybe he used to

live in a different town. Certainly he was once a child, but that was at a time when children were dressed like adults. You can see them like that in Granny's photograph album. In his room there are two chairs, a table, a carpet, a bed and a wardrobe. An alarm clock stands on a little table, next to it lie old newspapers, and the photograph album, a mirror and a picture hang on the wall.

In the morning the old man took a walk, and another in the afternoon, exchanging a few words with his neighbour, and in the evening he sat at his table.

This never changed, even on Sundays it was the same. And when the man sat at the table he heard the alarm clock tick, always he heard the alarm clock tick.

Then suddenly came a special day, a day with sunshine, not too hot, not too cold, with birds twittering, with friendly people, with children who were playing – and the special thing about it was that for once it all pleased the man.

He smiled.

"Now everything is going to change," he thought. He undid his top shirt button, seized his hat, accelerated his pace, went so far as to make his knees flex as he walked, and was glad. He came back to his street, nodded to the children, walked up to his house, climbed the stairs, took his keys out of his pocket and unlocked his room.

But in his room everything was the same, a table, two

chairs, a bed. And as he sat down he heard that ticking again, and all the gladness went out of him, for nothing had changed.

And a great rage took possession of the man.

In the mirror he saw his face flush, as he narrowed his eyes; then he clenched his hands, raised them and brought them down on the table-top, only one blow at first, then another, and then he started to drum on the table, while he cried out again and again:

"It's got to change, it's got to change."

And he no longer heard the alarm clock. Then his hands began to hurt, his voice failed, then he heard the alarm clock again and nothing changed.

"Always the same table," said the man, "the same chairs, the bed, the picture. And the table I call table, the picture I call picture, the bed is called bed, and the chair is called chair. Why, come to think of it? The French call a bed 'lee', a table 'tahbl', call a picture 'tahblow' and a chair 'shaze', and they understand each other. And the Chinese understand each other too."

"Why isn't the bed called picture?" thought the man, and smiled, then he laughed, laughed till the neighbours banged on the wall and shouted "Quiet!"

"Now things are going to change," he cried out, and from now on he called the bed 'picture'.

"I'm tired, I want to go to picture," he said, and often in the morning he would lie in picture for a long time, wondering what he would now call the chair, and he called the chair 'alarm clock'.

So he got up, dressed, sat down on his alarm clock and rested his arms on the table. But the table was no longer called table, it was now called carpet. So in the morning the man left his picture, got dressed, sat down at the carpet on the alarm clock and wondered what to call what.

He called the bed picture.

He called the table carpet.

He called the chair alarm clock.

He called the newspaper bed.

He called the mirror chair.

He called the alarm clock photograph album.

He called the wardrobe newspaper.

He called the carpet wardrobe.

He called the picture table.

And he called the photograph album mirror.

So:

In the morning the old man would lie in picture for a long time, at nine the photograph album rang, the man got up and stood on the wardrobe, so that his feet wouldn't feel cold, then he took his clothes out of the newspaper, dressed, looked into the chair on the wall, then sat down on the alarm clock at the carpet and turned the pages of the mirror until he found his mother's table.

The man thought this was fun, and he practised all day long and impressed the words on his memory. Now he gave everything new names. Now he was no longer a man, but a foot, and the foot was a morning and the morning a man.

Now you can continue the story for yourselves. And then, like the man, you can change the other words round:

to ring is to stand,
to feel cold is to look,
to lie is to ring,
to get up is to feel cold,
to stand is to turn over the pages.
So we get this:

In the man the old foot would ring in picture for a long time, at nine the photograph album stood, the foot felt cold and turned over the pages on the wardrobe, so that his mornings would not look.

The old man bought himself blue exercise books and filled them with the new words, and it kept him very busy, and now he was rarely seen in the street.

Then he learned the new names for all kinds of things and forgot the right ones more and more. He now had a new language that belonged to him alone.

Now and again he began to dream in the new language, and then he translated the songs of his school days into his own language and sang them softly to himself.

But soon even translating became difficult for him, he had almost forgotten his old language, and he had to look for the right words in his blue exercise books. And he was frightened of talking to people. He had to search his mind for a long time for the names that people call things.

His picture people call bed.
His carpet people call table.
His alarm clock people call chair.
His bed people call newspaper.
His chair people call mirror.
His photograph album people call alarm clock.
His newspaper people call wardrobe.
His wardrobe people call carpet.
His table people call picture.
His mirror people call photograph album. And it went

so far that the man couldn't help laughing when he heard people talk.

He couldn't help laughing when he heard someone say:

"Will you be going to the football match tomorrow?" Or when someone said: "It's been raining for two months." Or when someone said: "I've got an uncle in America."

He couldn't help laughing because he didn't understand a word of it.

But this is not a cheerful story. It began sadly and ends sadly too.

The old man in the grey coat couldn't understand people any more; that wasn't so bad.

What was much worse, they couldn't understand him any more.

And that's why he gave up talking.

He kept quiet, spoke only to himself, no longer so much as nodded to people when he passed them.

Peter Bischel

Translated from the German by **Michael Hamburger**

How the Cat Became

Things were running very smoothly and most of the
creatures were highly pleased with themselves. Lion was
already famous. Even the little shrews and moles and
spiders were pretty well known.

But among all these busy creatures there was one who
seemed to be getting nowhere. It was Cat.

Cat was a real oddity. The others didn't know what to
make of him at all.

He lived in a hollow tree in the wood. Every night,
when the rest of the creatures were sound asleep, he
retired to the depths of his tree – then such sounds, such
screechings, yowlings, wailings! The bats that slept upside-
down all day long in the hollows of the tree branches
awoke with a start and fled with their wing-tips stuffed
into their ears. It seemed to them that Cat was having the
worst nightmares ever – ten at a time.

But no. Cat was tuning his violin.

If only you could have seen him! Curled in the warm
smooth hollow of his tree, gazing up through the hole at
the top of the trunk, smiling at the stars, winking at the
moon – his violin tucked under his chin. Ah, Cat was a
happy one.

And all night long he sat there composing his tunes.

Now the creatures didn't like this at all. They saw no

use in his music, it made
no food, it built no nest,
it didn't even keep him
warm. And the way Cat
lounged around all day,
sleeping in the sun, was
just more than they
could stand.

"He's a bad example,"
said Beaver, "he never
does a stroke of work! What if our children think they can
live as idly as he does?"

"It's time," said Weasel, "that Cat had a job like
everybody else in the world."

So the creatures of the wood formed a Committee to
persuade Cat to take a job.

Jay, Magpie, and Parrot went along at dawn and sat in
the topmost twigs of Cat's old tree. As soon as Cat poked
his head out, they all began together:

"You've to get a job. Get a job! Get a job!"

That was only the beginning of it. All day long,
everywhere he went, those birds were at him:

"Get a job! Get a job!"

And try as he would, Cat could not get a wink of sleep.

That night he went back to his tree early. He was far
too tired to practise on his violin and fell fast asleep in a
few minutes. Next morning, when he poked his head out

of the tree at first light, the three birds of the Committee were there again, loud as ever:

"Get a job!"

Cat ducked back down into his tree and began to think. He wasn't going to start grubbing around in the wet woods all day, as they wanted him to. Oh no. He wouldn't have any time to play his violin if he did that. There was only one thing to do and he did it.

He tucked his violin under his arm and suddenly jumped out at the top of the tree and set off through the woods at a run. Behind him, shouting and calling, came Jay, Magpie, and Parrot.

Other creatures that were about their daily work in the undergrowth looked up when Cat ran past. No one had ever seen Cat run before.

"Cat's up to something," they called to each other. "Maybe he's going to get a job at last."

Deer, Wild Boar, Bear, Ferret, Mongoose, Porcupine, and a cloud of birds set off after Cat to see where he was going.

After a great deal of running they came to the edge of the forest. There they stopped. As they peered through the leaves they looked sideways at each other and trembled. Ahead of them, across an open field covered with haycocks, was Man's farm.

But Cat wasn't afraid. He went straight on, over the field, and up to Man's door. He raised his paw and banged as hard as he could in the middle of the door.

Man was so surprised to see Cat that at first he just stood, eyes wide, mouth open. No creature ever dared to come on to his fields, let alone knock at his door. Cat spoke first.

"I've come for a job," he said.

"A job?" asked Man, hardly able to believe his ears.

"Work," said Cat. "I want to earn my living."

Man looked him up and down, then saw his long claws.

"You look as if you'd make a fine rat-catcher," said Man.

Cat was surprised to hear that. He wondered what it was about him that made him look like a rat-catcher. Still, he wasn't going to miss the chance of a job. So he stuck out his chest and said: "Been doing it for years."

"Well then, I've a job for you," said Man. "My farm's swarming with rats and mice. They're in my haystacks, they're in my corn sacks, and they're all over the pantry."

So before Cat knew where he was, he had been signed on as a Rat-and-Mouse-Catcher. His pay was milk, and meat, and a place at the fireside. He slept all day and worked all night.

At first he had a terrible time. The rats pulled his tail, the mice nipped his ears. They climbed on to rafters above him and dropped down — thump! on to him in the dark. They teased the life out of him.

18

But Cat was a quick learner. At the end of the week he could lay out a dozen rats and twice as many mice within half an hour. If he'd gone on laying them out all night there would pretty soon have been none left, and Cat would have been out of a job. So he just caught a few each night – in the first ten minutes or so. Then he retired into the barn and played his violin till morning. This was just the job he had been looking for.

Man was delighted with him. And Mrs Man thought he was beautiful. She took him on to her lap and stroked him for hours on end. What a life! thought Cat. If only those silly creatures in the dripping wet woods could see him now!

Well, when the other farmers saw what a fine rat-and-mouse-catcher Cat was, they all wanted cats too. Soon there were so many cats that our Cat decided to form a string band. Oh yes, they were all great violinists. Every night, after making one pile of rats and another of mice, each cat left his farm and was away over the fields to a little dark spinney.

Then what tunes! All night long…

Pretty soon lady cats began to arrive. Now, every night, instead of just music, there was dancing too. And what dances! If only you could have crept up there and peeped into the glade from behind a tree and seen the cats dancing – the glossy furred ladies and the tomcats, some pearly grey, some ginger red, and all with wonderful green flashing eyes. Up and down the glade, with the music flying out all over the night.

At dawn they hung their violins in the larch trees, dashed back to the farms, and pretended they had been working all night among the rats and mice. They lapped their milk hungrily, stretched out at the fireside, and fell asleep with smiles on their faces.

Ted Hughes

Return to Air

The Ponds are very big, so that at one end people bathe and at the other end they fish. Old chaps with bald heads sit on folding stools and fish with rods and lines, and little kids squeeze through the railings and wade out into the water to fish with nets. But the water's much deeper at our end of the Ponds, and that's where we bathe. You're not allowed to bathe there unless you can swim; but I've always been able to swim. They used to say that was because fat floats – well, I don't mind. They call me Sausage.

Only, I don't dive – not from any diving-board, thank you. I have to take my glasses off to go into the water, and I can't see without them, and I'm just not going to dive, even from the lowest diving-board, and that's that, and they stopped nagging about it long ago.

Then, this summer, they were all on to me to learn duck-diving. You're swimming on the surface of the water and suddenly you up-end yourself just like a duck and dive down deep into the water, and perhaps you swim about a bit underwater, and then come up again. I daresay ducks begin doing it soon after they're born. It's different for them.

So I was learning to duck-dive – to swim down to the bottom of the Ponds, and pick up a brick they'd thrown in, and bring it up again. You practise that in case you have to rescue anyone from drowning – say, they'd sunk for the third time and gone to the bottom. Of course, they'd be bigger and heavier than a brick, but I suppose you have to begin with bricks and work up gradually to people.

The swimming-instructor said, "Sausage, I'm going to throw the brick in –" It was a brick with a bit of old white flannel round it, to make it show up under-water. "– Sausage, I'm going to throw it in, and you go *after* it – go *after* it, Sausage, and get it before it reaches the bottom and settles in the mud, or you'll never get it."

He'd made everyone come out of the water to give me a chance, and they were standing watching. I could see them blurred along the bank, and I could hear them talking and laughing; but there wasn't a sound in the water except me just treading water gently, waiting. And then I saw the brick go over my head as the instructor threw it, and there was a splash as it went into the water ahead of me; and I thought: I can't do it – my legs won't up-end this time – they feel just flabby – they'll float, but they won't up-end – they can't up-end – it's different for ducks… But while I was thinking all that, I'd taken a deep breath, and then my head really went down and my legs went up into the air – I could feel them there, just air around them, and then there was water round them, because I was going down into the water, after all. Right down into the water; straight down…

At first my eyes were shut, although I didn't know I'd shut them. When I did realize, I forced my eyelids up against the water to see. Because, although I can't see much without my glasses, as I've said, I don't believe anyone could see much under-water in those Ponds; so I could see as much as anyone.

The water was like a thick greeny-brown lemonade, with wispy little things moving very slowly about in it – or perhaps they were just movements of the water, not things at all; I couldn't tell. The brick had a few seconds' start of me, of course, but I could still see a whitish glimmer that must be the flannel round it: it was ahead of me, fading away into the lower water, as I moved after it.

The funny thing about swimming under-water is its being so still and quiet and shady down there, after all the air and sunlight and splashing and shouting just up above. I was shut right in by the quiet, greeny-brown water, just me alone with the brick ahead of me, both of us making towards the bottom.

The Ponds are deep, but I knew they weren't too deep; and, of course, I knew I'd enough air in my lungs from the breath I'd taken. I knew all that.

Down we went, and the lemonade-look quite went from the water and it became just a dark blackish-brown,

and you'd wonder you could see anything at all.
Especially as the bit of white flannel seemed to have
come off the brick by the time it reached the bottom and
I'd caught up with it. The brick looked different down
there, anyway, and it had already settled right into the
mud – there was only one corner left sticking up.

I dug in the mud with my fingers and got hold of the
thing, and then I didn't think of anything except getting
up again with it into the air.

Touching the bottom like that had stirred up the mud,
so that I began going up through a thick cloud of it. I let
myself go up – they say fat floats, you know – but I was
shooting myself upwards too. I was in a hurry.

The funny thing was, I only began to be afraid when I
was going back. I suddenly thought: perhaps I've swum
under-water much too far – perhaps I'll come up at the
far end of the Ponds among all the fishermen and foul
their lines and perhaps get a fish-hook caught in the flesh
of my cheek. And all the time I was going up quite
quickly, and the water was changing from brown-black to
green-brown and then to bright lemonade. I could almost
see the sun shining through the water, I was so near the
surface. It wasn't until then that I felt really frightened:
I thought I was moving much too slowly and I'd never
reach the air again in time.

Never the air again…

Then suddenly I was at the surface – I'd exploded

24

back from the water into the air. For a while I couldn't think of anything and I couldn't do anything except let out the old breath I'd been holding and take a couple of fresh, quick ones, and tread water – and hang on to that brick.

Pond water was trickling down inside my nose and into my mouth, which I hate. But there was air all round and above, for me to breathe, to live.

And then I noticed they were shouting from the bank. They were cheering and shouting, "Sausage! Sausage!" and the instructor was hallooing with his hands round his mouth, and bellowing to me: "What on earth have you got there, Sausage?"

So then I turned myself properly round – I'd come up almost facing the fishermen at the other end of the Pond, but otherwise only a few feet from where I'd gone down; so that was all right. I turned round and swam to the bank and they hauled me out and gave me my glasses to have a good look at what I'd brought up from the bottom.

Because it wasn't a brick. It was just about the size and shape of one, but it was a tin – an old, old tin box with no paint left on it and all brown-black slime from the bottom of the Ponds. It was as heavy as a brick because it was full of mud. Don't get excited, as we did: there was nothing there but mud. We strained all the mud through our fingers, but there wasn't anything else there – not even a bit of old sandwich or the remains of bait. I thought there might have been, because the tin could have belonged to one of the old chaps that have always fished at the other end of the Ponds. They often bring their dinners with them in bags or tins, and they have tins for bait, too. It could have been dropped into the water at their end of the Ponds and got moved to our end with the movement of the water. Otherwise I don't know how that tin box can have got there. Anyway, it must have been there for years and years, by the look of it. When you think, it might have stayed there for years and years longer; perhaps stayed sunk under-water for ever.

I've cleaned the tin up and I keep it on the mantelpiece at home with my coin collection in it. I had to duck-dive later for another brick, and I got it all right, without being frightened at all; but it didn't seem to matter as much as coming up with the tin. I shall keep the tin as long as I live, and I might easily live to be a hundred.

Philippa Pearce

Chocolate Cake

I love chocolate cake.
And when I was a boy
I loved it even more.

Sometimes we used to have it for tea
and Mum used to say,
"If there's any left over
you can have it to take to school
tomorrow to have at playtime."
And the next day I would take it to school
wrapped up in tin foil
open it up at playtime and sit in the
corner of the playground
eating it,
you know how the icing on top
is all shiny and it cracks as you
bite into it
and there's that other kind of icing
in the middle
and it sticks to your hands and you can
lick your fingers
and lick your lips
oh it's lovely.
yeah.

Anyway,
once we had this chocolate cake for tea
and later I went to bed
but while I was in bed
I found myself waking up
licking my lips
and smiling.
I woke up proper.
"The chocolate cake."
It was the first thing
I thought of.
I could almost see it
so I thought,
what if I go downstairs
and have a little nibble, yeah?

It was all dark
everyone was in bed
so it must have been really late
but I got out of bed,
crept out of the door

there's always a creaky floorboard, isn't there?

Past Mum and Dad's room,

careful not to tread on bits of broken toys
or bits of Lego
you know what it's like treading on Lego
with your bare feet,

yowwww

shhhhhh

downstairs
into the kitchen
open the cupboard
and there it is
all shining.

So I take it out of the cupboard
put it on the table
and I see that
there's a few crumbs lying about on the plate,
so I lick my finger and run my finger all over the crumbs
scooping them up
and put them into my mouth.

oooooooommmmmmmmmm

nice.

Then
I look again
and on one side where it's been cut,
it's all crumbly.
So I take a knife
I think I'll just tidy that up a bit,
cut off the crumbly bits
scoop them all up
and into the mouth

oooooommm mmmm
nice.

Look at the cake again.

That looks a bit funny now,
one side doesn't match the other
I'll just even it up a bit, eh?

Take the knife
and slice.
This time the knife makes a little cracky noise
as it goes through that hard icing on top.

A whole slice this time,

into the mouth.
Oh the icing on top
and the icing in the middle
ohhhhhh oooo mmmmmm.

But now
I can't stop myself.
Knife –
I just take any old slice at it
and I've got this great big chunk
and I'm cramming it in
what a greedy pig
but it's so nice,

and there's another
and another and I'm squealing and I'm smacking my lips
and I'm stuffing myself with it
and
before I know
I've eaten the lot.

The whole lot.
I look at the plate.
It's all gone.

Oh no
they're bound to notice, aren't they,
a whole chocolate cake doesn't just disappear
does it?

What shall I do?

I know. I'll wash the plate up,
and the knife

and put them away and maybe no one
will notice, eh?

So I do that
and creep creep creep
back to bed
into bed
doze off
licking my lips

with a lovely feeling in my belly.
Mmmmmmmmmm.

In the morning I get up,
downstairs,
have breakfast,
Mum's saying,
"Have you got your dinner money?"
and I say,
"Yes."
"And don't forget to take some chocolate cake with you."
I stopped breathing.

"What's the matter," she says,
"you normally jump at chocolate cake?"

I'm still not breathing,
and she's looking at me very closely now.
She's looking at me just below my mouth.
"What's that?" she says.
"What's what?" I say.
"What's that there?"
"Where?"
"There," she says, pointing at my chin.
"I don't know," I say.
"It looks like chocolate," she says.
"It's not chocolate cake is it?"
No answer.
"Is it?"

32

"I don't know."
She goes to the cupboard
looks in, up, top, middle, bottom,
turns back to me.
"It's gone."
It's gone.
"You haven't eaten it, have you?"
"I don't know."
"You don't know? You don't know if you've eaten a whole
chocolate cake or not?
When? When did you eat it?"

So I told her,

and she said
well what could she say?
"That's the last time I give you any cake to take
to school.
Now go. Get out
no wait
not before you've washed your dirty sticky face."
I went upstairs
looked in the mirror
and there it was, just below my mouth,
a chocolate smudge.
The give-away.
Maybe she'll forget about it by next week.

Michael Rosen

The Stowaways

When I lived in Liverpool, my best friend was a boy
called Midge. Kevin Midgeley was his real name, but we
called him Midge for short. And he was short, only about
three cornflake boxes high (empty ones at that). No three
ways about it. Midge was my best friend and we had lots
of things in common. Things we enjoyed doing like …
climbing trees, playing footy, going to the movies, hitting
each other really hard. And there were things we didn't
enjoy doing like … sums, washing behind our ears, eating
cabbage.

But there was one thing that really bound us together,
one thing we had in common – a love of the sea.

In the old days (but not so long ago), the river Mersey
was far busier than it is today. Those were the days of the

great passenger liners and cargo boats. Large ships sailed out of Liverpool for Canada, the United States, South Africa, the West Indies, all over the world. My father had been to sea and so had all my uncles, and my grandfather. Six foot six, muscles rippling in the wind, huge hands grappling with the helm, rum-soaked and fierce as a wounded shark (and that was only my grandmother!) By the time they were twenty, most young men in this city had visited parts of the globe I can't even spell.

In my bedroom each night, I used to lie in bed (best place to lie really), I used to lie there, especially in winter, and listen to the foghorns being sounded all down the river. I could picture the ship nosing its way out of the docks into the channel and out into the Irish Sea. It was exciting. All those exotic places. All those exciting adventures.

Midge and I knew what we wanted to do when we left school … become sailors. A captain, an admiral, perhaps one day even a steward. Of course we were only about seven or eight at the time so we thought we'd have a long time to wait. But oddly enough, the call of the sea came sooner than we'd expected.

It was a Wednesday if I remember rightly. I never liked Wednesdays for some reason. I could never spell it for a start and it always seemed to be raining, and there were still two days to go before the weekend. Anyway, Midge and I got into trouble at school. I don't remember what for (something trivial I suppose like chewing gum in class, forgetting how to read, setting fire to the music teacher), I forget now. But we were picked on, nagged, told off and all those boring things that grown-ups get up to sometimes.

And, of course, to make matters worse, my mum and dad were in a right mood when I got home. Nothing to do with me, of course, because as you have no doubt gathered by now, I was the perfect child: clean, well-mannered, obedient ... soft in the head. But for some reason I was clipped round the ear and sent to bed early for being childish. Childish! I ask you. I *was* a child. A child acts his age, what does he get? Wallop!

So that night in bed, I decided ... Yes, you've guessed it. I could hear the big ships calling out to each other as they sidled out of the Mersey into the oceans beyond. The tugs leading the way like proud little guide dogs. That's it. We'd run away to sea, Midge and I. I'd tell him the good news in the morning.

The next two days just couldn't pass quickly enough for us. We had decided to begin our amazing around-the-world voyage on Saturday morning so that in case we didn't like it we would be back in time for school on Monday. As you can imagine there was a lot to think about – what clothes to take, how much food and drink. We decided on two sweaters each and wellies in case we ran into storms around Cape Horn. I read somewhere

36

that sailors lived off rum and dry biscuits, so I poured some of my dad's into an empty pop bottle, and borrowed a handful of half-coated chocolate digestives. I also packed my lonestar cap gun and Midge settled on a magnifying glass.

On Friday night we met round at his house to make the final plans. He lived with his granny and his sister, so there were no nosy parents to discover what we were up to. We hid all the stuff in the shed in the yard and arranged to meet outside his back door next morning at the crack of dawn, or sunrise – whichever came first.

Sure enough, Saturday morning, when the big finger was on twelve and the little one was on six, Midge and I met with our little bundles under our arms and ran up the street as fast as our tiptoes could carry us.

Hardly anyone was about, and the streets were so quiet and deserted except for a few pigeons straddling home after all-night parties. It was a very strange feeling, as if we were the only people alive and the city belonged entirely to us. And soon the world would be ours as well – once we'd stowed away on a ship bound for somewhere far off and exciting.

By the time we'd got down to the Pier Head, though, a lot more people were up and about, including a policeman who eyed us suspiciously. "Ello, Ello, Ello," he said, "and where are you two going so early in the morning?"

"Fishing," I said.

"Train spotting," said Midge and we looked at each other.

"Just so long as you're not running away to sea."

"Oh no," we chorused. "Just as if."

He winked at us. "Off you go then, and remember to look both ways before crossing your eyes."

We ran off and straight down on to the landing stage where a lot of ships were tied up. There was no time to lose because already quite a few were putting out to sea, their sirens blowing, the hundreds of seagulls squeaking excitedly, all tossed into the air like giant handfuls of confetti.

Then I noticed a small ship just to the left where the crew were getting ready to cast off. They were so busy doing their work that it was easy for Midge and me to slip on board unnoticed. Up the gang-plank we went and straight up on to the top deck where there was nobody around. The sailors were all busy down below, hauling in the heavy ropes and revving up the engine that turned the great propellers.

We looked around for somewhere to hide. "I know, let's climb down the funnel," said Midge.

"Great idea," I said, taking the mickey. "Or, better still, let's disguise ourselves as a pair of seagulls and perch up there on the mast."

Then I spotted them. The lifeboats. "Quick, let's climb

into one of those, they'll never look in there – not unless we run into icebergs anyway." So in we climbed, and no sooner had we covered ourselves with the tarpaulin than there was a great shuddering and the whole ship seemed to turn round on itself. We were off! Soon we'd be digging for diamonds in the Brazilian jungle or building sandcastles on a tropical island. But we had to be patient, we knew that. Those places are a long way away, it could take days, even months.

So we were patient. Very patient. Until after what seemed like hours and hours we decided to eat our rations, which I divided up equally. I gave Midge all the rum and I had all the biscuits. Looking back on it now, that probably wasn't a good idea, especially for Midge.

What with the rolling of the ship and not having had any breakfast, and the excitement, and a couple of swigs of rum - well you can guess what happened – woooorrppp!

All over the place. We pulled back the sheet and decided to give ourselves up. We were too far away at sea now for the captain to turn back. The worst he could do was to clap us in irons or shiver our timbers.

We climbed down on to the deck and as Midge staggered to the nearest rail to feed the fishes, I looked out to sea hoping to catch sight of a whale, a shoal of dolphins, perhaps see the coast of America coming in to view. And what did I see? The Liver Buildings.

Anyone can make a mistake can't they? I mean, we weren't to know we'd stowed away on a ferryboat.

One that goes from Liverpool to Birkenhead and back again, toing and froing across the Mersey. We'd done four trips hidden in the lifeboat and ended up back in Liverpool. And we'd only been away about an hour and a half. "Ah well, so much for running away to sea," we thought as we disembarked (although disembowelled might be a better word as far as Midge was concerned). Rum? Yuck.

We got the bus home. My mum and dad were having their breakfast. "Aye, aye," said my dad, "here comes the early bird. And what have you been up to then?"

"I ran away to sea," I said.

"Mm, that's nice," said my mum, shaking out the cornflakes. "That's nice."

Roger McGough

40

The Fun They Had

Margie even wrote about it that night in her diary. On the page headed May 17, 2157, she wrote, "Today Tommy found a real book!"

It was a very old book. Margie's grandfather once said that when he was a little boy *his* grandfather told him that there was a time when all stories were printed on paper.

They turned the pages, which were yellow and crinkly, and it was awfully funny to read words that stood still instead of moving the way they were supposed to – on a screen, you know. And then, when they turned back to the page before, it had the same words on it that it had had when they read it the first time.

"Gee," said Tommy, "what a waste. When you're through with the book, you just throw it away, I guess. Our television screen must have had a million books on it, and it's good for plenty more. I wouldn't throw it away."

"Same as mine," said Margie. She was eleven and hadn't seen as many textbooks as Tommy had. He was thirteen.

She said, "Where did you find it?"

"In my house." He pointed without looking, because he was busy reading. "In the attic."

41

"What's it about?"

"School."

Margie was scornful. "School? What's there to write about school? I hate school."

Margie always hated school, but now she hated it more than ever. The mechanical teacher had been giving her test after test in geography, and she had been doing worse and worse until her mother had shaken her head sorrowfully and sent for the County Inspector.

He was a round little man with a red face and a whole box of tools with dials and wires. He smiled at Margie and gave her an apple, then took the teacher apart. Margie had hoped he wouldn't know how to put it together again, but he knew how all right, and, after an hour or so, there it was again, large and black and ugly, with a big screen on which all the lessons were shown and the questions were asked. That wasn't so bad. The part Margie hated most was the slot where she had to put homework and test papers. She always had to write them out in a punch code they made her learn when she was six years old, and the mechanical teacher calculated the mark in no time.

The Inspector had smiled after he was finished and patted Margie's head. He said to her mother, "It's not the little girl's fault, Mrs. Jones. I think the geography sector was geared a little too quick. Those things happen sometimes. I've slowed it up to an average ten-year level.

Actually, the overall pattern of her progress is quite satisfactory." And he patted Margie's head again.

Margie was disappointed. She had been hoping they would take the teacher away altogether. They had once taken Tommy's teacher away for nearly a month because the history sector had blanked out completely.

So she said to Tommy, "Why would anyone write about school?"

Tommy looked at her with very superior eyes. "Because it's not our kind of school, stupid. This is the old kind of school that they had hundreds and hundreds of years ago." He added loftily, pronouncing the word carefully, "*Centuries* ago."

Margie was hurt. "Well, I don't know what kind of school they had all that time ago." She read the book over his shoulder for a while, then said, "Anyway, they had a teacher."

"Sure they had a teacher, but it wasn't a *regular* teacher. It was a man."

"A man? How could a man be a teacher?"

"Well, he just told the boys and girls things and gave them homework and asked them questions."

"A man isn't smart enough."

"Sure he is. My father knows as much as my teacher."

"He can't. A man can't know as much as a teacher."

"He knows almost as much, I betcha."

Margie wasn't prepared to dispute that. She said,

"I wouldn't want a strange man in my house to teach me."

Tommy screamed with laughter. "You don't know much, Margie. The teachers didn't live in the house. They had a special building and all the kids went there."

"And all the kids learned the same thing?"

"Sure, if they were the same age."

"But my mother says a teacher has to be adjusted to fit the mind of each boy and girl it teaches and that each kid has to be taught differently."

"Just the same, they didn't do it that way then. If you don't like it, you don't have to read the book."

"I didn't say I didn't like it," Margie said quickly. She wanted to read about those funny schools.

They weren't even half-finished when Margie's mother called, "Margie! School!"

Margie looked up. "Not yet, Mamma."

"Now!" said Mrs. Jones. "And it's probably time for Tommy, too."

Margie said to Tommy, "Can I read the book some more with you after school?"

"Maybe," he said nonchalantly. He walked away whistling, the dusty old book tucked beneath his arm.

Margie went into the schoolroom. It was right next to her bedroom, and the mechanical teacher was on and waiting for her. It was always on at the same time every day except Saturday and Sunday, because her mother said little girls learned better if they learned at regular hours.

The screen was lit up, and it said, "Today's arithmetic lesson is on the addition of proper fractions. Please insert yesterday's homework in the proper slot."

Margie did so with a sigh. She was thinking about the old schools they had when her grandfather's grandfather was a little boy. All the kids from the whole neighborhood came, laughing and shouting in the schoolyard, sitting together in the same schoolroom, going home together at the end of the day. They learned the same things, so they could help one another on the homework and talk about it.

And the teachers were people...

The mechanical teacher was flashing on the screen: "When we add the fractions $\frac{1}{2}$ and $\frac{1}{4}$ – "

Margie was thinking about how the kids must have loved it in the old days. She was thinking about the fun they had.

Isaac Asimov

The Shoppers

In the first shop they bought a packet of dogseed, because Doreen had always wanted to grow her own dog. In the second, a pair of bird shoes, which fluttered slightly as Matthew put them on. In the third shop, Little Tommy bought half a dozen singing biscuits, five of which he swallowed straight away, because shopping made him hungry.

There were only nine shops in the entire city. In fact, the shops *were* the city, so vast they were and all encompassing. It was difficult to know where one shop ended and the next began. No wonder the children were tired already.

In the fourth shop Doreen chose a box of shadows, some of which she used to mask the pain in the head that Tommy's constant singing gave her. In the fifth shop, Matthew floated over the umbrella-pig cage in his bird shoes, claiming that if Doreen had bought the shadows, then he should have at least a *single* pig to keep the rain off. Doreen reminded him it never rained inside the shops, and that he should instead buy an egg of words. Matthew was becoming angry at the way this shopping trip was going.

The three young shoppers were determined to buy a single product from each of the nine stores. These precious items were to be the children's gift to their mother, for her birthday. Their mother, you see, had never once ventured outside the first shop.

In shop six, Tommy bought a penny ghost. In shop seven, Doreen purchased a Girl-of-Eternal-Flame Doll. In shop number eight, Matthew wanted to buy a genuine piece of cow, but Doreen told him they could no longer afford it. Instead, he was forced to buy a mansion house in London. In the ninth and final shop, Little Tommy bought a smoke-map of Manchester, which they used to retrace their steps through the aisles of the city.

On the way home, however, the dogseeds slipped from Doreen's fingers, caught on a slight breeze. The bird shoes tried to catch the seeds, only to crash into a display stand, tumbling poor Matthew to the ground. He landed on Tommy, who swallowed his last song biscuit accidentally. Doreen used many more of her shadows to wipe away Tommy's wailing. Matthew's egg hatched prematurely in his pocket. The resulting cloud of words gathered over the Flame Doll, forming the word 'locust' in the air. The doll ran screaming into the mansion house, shooting electric sparks from her hair. The house burned so fiercely that not even the fire brigade could put it out. They'd forgotten to bring their hosepipes.

Tommy smoked his map completely to get them home to Mother's little kiosk. All that remained was the penny ghost and a single shadow. The children were in tears by then, but their mother accepted gratefully the gift of the shadow and told Little Tommy he could keep the ghost for his trouble and kindness. That night he played with the spirit, as his mother wiped her sad eyes with the birthday shadow and told them the story of the mythical tenth shop, the one that lay beyond all the others.

Jeff Noon

The Pirate's Dagger

Last Saturday, we went to the auction with Granpa. We hadn't been there for months, Kit and me. We knew exactly what to expect, though. For instance, Granpa began as he always does by picking his favourite bidding-card: number 505.

It's his lucky card, he says.

After that, he took his usual walk round the huge, crowded hall looking hard at everything there.

"You never know what you might find," he told us. "Most of it's junk, of course. But every so often you'll come across *treasure*!"

"Oh yeah?" yawned Kit.

"You say that every time," I sighed.

Granpa winked and tapped his nose. "Lads, there's bound to be treasure here somewhere. Why else would you get so many dealers in a place like this? They're looking for just the right stuff to sell in the posh antique shops."

Up on his podium, the auctioneer banged his hammer. "Everyone ready?" he asked. "Two hundred items an hour we've got to get through. So let's get a wiggle on, folks."

Then he was off. How could he talk so fast in such a loud voice? "First lot today – oil painting, man in an armchair. Five pounds I'm offered – seven over here. Eight with me. Ten there at the back…come on, the frame's worth more than that. Twelve with me. Fourteen at the back. It's out now. Sixteen I'm after. Are we all done? Gone for fourteen pounds."

BANG went his hammer. "Number 747," he told his assistant as the winning-bidder held up her card.

It took about fifteen seconds altogether. You have to be really quick at an auction. You have to understand the language, too. When the auctioneer says "with me" he means the bids he was given before the auction started. "It's out now" means he's gone beyond these bids so the next bid could be the winner. And when he says "are we all done?" it means he's about to bring down his hammer.

Simple, really.

Also rather boring if you've seen it before. My head began to nod, I admit. Goodness knows how long I'd been dozing when Kit jabbed me in the ribs. "Hey, Pete," he whispered, pointing at something in the catalogue. "Get a load of this!"

I looked down, bleary-eyed.

Lot 143, it said. *Rep. Pirate's Dagger (£5–£10)*

"Is that treasure or what?" Kit hissed.

"It's treasure, definitely," I gulped. "Has Granpa seen it? Get him to put in a bid!"

"He's just gone off to the loo, Pete. And you know how long that takes him. We're on Lot 142 already. Granpa will never be back in time. Here, you do the bidding for him!"

"Why not you?"

"Because I said it first, that's why."

He'd got me there, of course. If I copped out now, he'd tease me for ever and ever.

"Lot 143," the auctioneer announced. "Rep. Pirate's dagger. Good condition, this. Five pounds I'm offered – ten at the back, with the gent in the leather overcoat. Fifteen with me. Looking for twenty…twenty I have at the back. It's out now. Looking for twenty-five…"

"Quick!" Kit yelped.

I thrust Granpa's bidding-card in the air. The auctioneer saw it at once. "New bidder to the left," he said. "Twenty-five it is. Looking for thirty. Thirty at the back with the leather overcoat. Looking for thirty-five…"

"Pete…" Kit nudged me.

My hand flew up again. "Thirty five to the left," called the auctioneer. "Forty at the back."

"Pete…"

"Forty-five to the left. Looking for fifty…yes, fifty at the back. Fifty-five to the left. Looking for sixty now…no offer at sixty? Not from you, sir, in the leather overcoat? Are we all done, then?"

BANG!

"Gone for fifty-five pounds to Card 505 – the young gent bidding for his Granpa," the auctioneer smiled.

Suddenly, Kit and I realised what we'd done. For one thing, we'd just paid fifty-five pounds for a lot valued at £5–£10. For another, fifty-five pounds was about half Granpa's pension for the week. Worst of all, though, we'd both remembered that 'rep' is short for 'replica'. This is a fancy word for 'fake'.

Honestly, we wanted to die.

So we were amazed by Granpa's reaction when the auction was over. "Forget it, lads," he said with a shrug. "You've just learned an important lesson: never get over-excited at an auction. Especially if you think you've discovered treasure!"

He held up the pirate's dagger. Somehow, it looked more of a fake than ever outside in the sunlight. Or it did to us at any rate. The man who tapped Granpa's shoulder had a different opinion. It was the bidder in the leather overcoat. With his long greasy hair, he looked a bit like a pirate himself. "You're a dealer, aren't you?" he growled.

"Me?" said Granpa.

"Yes, you."

His glare as he stared at Granpa, was enough to make anyone walk the plank. "Clever that," he went on. "Getting these kids here to do your bidding for you. Made me give up much too soon. I need that dagger for my collection. Fifty-five quid you gave for it, right? Well, I'll give you seventy-five right now."

"Seventy-five quid?" Granpa gasped.

The man in the leather overcoat gave a snort of disgust. "You dealers are all alike, aren't you. Okay, make it a hundred quid cash-in-hand. That's my final offer."

Granpa took the money, you can bet. Later, while we were having a pizza to celebrate, we laughed a lot about replicas, and Granpa's lucky card, and getting over-excited at auctions. Only afterwards did it cross my mind that greasy hair and a leather overcoat might be a perfect disguise for a dealer looking for treasure...

Since then, if I pass a posh antique shop, I always look in the window in case there's a pirate's dagger for sale.

Chris Powling

Room for One More

How difficult it was to sleep in that strange bed! She wrestled with the duvet and thumped the pillow; she turned her back on the flimsy curtains; she wished she had never come up to London.

At midnight she heard the grandfather clock whirr and strike; and then she heard the gravel in the driveway crunch. At once she jumped out of bed and crossed the room and just peeped between the curtains.

What she could see was a gleaming black hearse. But there was no coffin it, and no flowers. No, the hearse was packed out with living people: a crush of talking, laughing, living people.

Then the driver of the hearse looked straight up at her, as she peeped between the curtains.

"There's room for one more." That's what he said. She could hear his voice quite clearly. Then she tugged the curtains so they crossed over, and ran back across the room, and jumped into bed, and pulled the duvet up over her head. And when she woke up next morning, she really wasn't sure whether it was all a dream or not.

That day, she went shopping. In the big store, she did Levi's Jeanswear on the fifth floor; she did Adidas Sportwear and that was on the sixth floor; and then she did cosmetics and that was on the seventh floor. Carrying two bags in each hand, she walked over to the lift. But when the bell pinged and the doors opened, she saw the lift was already jammed full with people.

The lift attendant looked straight at her as she stood there with her bags. "There's room for one more," he said. And his face was the face of the driver of the hearse.

"No," she said quickly. "No, I'll walk down."

Then the lift door closed with a clang. At once there was a kind of grating screech, and a terrible rattling, then a huge double thud.

The lift in the big store dropped from top to bottom of the shaft, and every single person in it was killed.

Kevin Crossley-Holland

Visiting Mr Wade

Kit took a deep breath. If he didn't go down the alley soon, Mum would be coming out to look for him – or even worse, she'd send his brother Pete to find out why he was taking so long. "What are you hanging about for?" Pete would say. "Scared of Mr Wade, are you?"

And he'd see at once it was true and never let Kit forget it. Being teased by Pete was as bad as visiting Mr Wade. Well, nearly.

Kit thought of the last time he'd been down the alley. It was easy then because Mum was with him. She'd done all the talking in a voice that was gentle and friendly – not at all the way she spoke to him and Pete. "How are you today, Mr Wade? The shoes are ready, are they? Ah yes, here's the price chalked on the sole. Thank you, Mr Wade. You've done a lovely job as usual."

Was Mum frightened of the shoe mender as well, Kit wondered.

Most people were, after all, because Mr Wade had only half a face. He wore special glasses to hide this, one side normal and the other side bulging with a wobbly, glittery false eye. "Know what he does with it at night?" Pete whispered. "He bounces it up and down on the end of a bit of elastic, like a yo-yo!"

56

"You're horrible!" Kit protested.

"Me?" said Pete. "Mr Wade's eye is, you mean." And he held up his hand with fingers cupped into an eye-shape pointing this way and that like a periscope.

Which explained why Kit was still dithering at the entrance to the alley where Mr Wade had his shed. You don't have to worry yet, Kit told himself desperately, not even when you're in his back yard. He always stays in the hut, working, doesn't he? So before he could lose his nerve, Kit sprinted along the track between the houses, skidded to a halt at Mr Wade's back gate, lifted the latch, slipped inside and swung the gate shut behind him, all in a moment.

One of his last moments alive, maybe.

For Mr Wade wasn't in his shed at all. He was just across the yard, bending over a cucumber frame. At the click of the latch, he'd gone rigid.

57

Kit was rigid too. He knew there was no move he could make – even blinking was beyond him. He'd have to go on looking while Mr Wade slowly turned half a face towards him, the false eye jiggling in its socket. Kit would be the first kid in the world to see it in broad daylight.

Except Mr Wade didn't turn round.

Instead he straightened up and took a step to one side, careful to keep his back to Kit. Then came another step, then another – sideways like a crab. When he got to the shed door, he opened it and stepped through still sideways, still making sure there was no chance at all Kit would see a yo-yo eye in half a face.

Kit stared at the shed door. Mr Wade was safe enough now he was back in his shadowy workshop. The problem would come after Kit crossed the yard, went inside and handed over the shoes he'd brought for mending. How could he get his voice to sound as gentle and friendly as Mum's?

Chris Powling

Sea Tongue

Author's note: The tale was collected from Norfolk fishermen in 1905 and 1928 by the Reverend John Tongue, who was at one time Vicar of Mundesley. The tale of a church bell or bells pealing under the water is common to several places along the Norfolk and Suffolk coast, including Dunwich, as well as to Cardigan Bay and the Lancashire coast.

I see my 'fractured narrative' as a kind of sound-story for different voices (or for one voice taking the different parts). The form of the story owes something to the idea that everything in our universe, every stick and stone, has its own voice.

I am the bell. I'm the tongue of the bell. I was cast before your grandmother was a girl. Before your grandmother's grandmother. So long ago.

Listen now! I'm like to last. I'm gold and green, cast in bronze, I weigh two tons. Up here, in the belfry of this closed church, I'm surrounded by sounds. Mouthfuls of air. Words ring me.

High on this crumbling cliff, I can see the fields of spring and summer corn; they're green and gold, as I am. I can see

59

the shining water, silver and black, and the far fisherman on it. And look! Here comes the bellringer – the old bellwoman.

✳ ✶ ✳

I am the bellwoman. For as long as I live I'll ring this old bell for those who will listen.

Not the church people: they have all gone. Not the seabirds; not the lugworms; not the inside-out crabs nor the shining mackerel. Whenever storms shatter the glass or fogs take me by the throat, I ring for the sailor and the fisherman. I warn them off the quicksands and away from the crumbling cliff. I ring and save them from the sea-god.

✳ ✶ ✳

I am the sea-god. My body is dark; it's so bright you can scarcely look at me, so deep you cannot fathom me.

My clothing is salt-fret raised by the four winds, twisting shreds of mist, shining gloom. And fog, fog, proofed and damp and cold. I'll wrap them around the fisherman. I'll wreck his boat.

I remember the days when I ruled earth. I ruled her all – every grain and granule – and I'll rule her again. I'll gnaw at this crumbling cliff tonight. I'll undermine the church and its graveyard. I'll chew on the bones of the dead.

✳ ✶ ✳

We are the dead. We died in bed, we died on the sword, we fell out of the sky, we swallowed the ocean.

To come to this: this green graveyard with its rows of narrow beds. Each of us separate and all of us one.

We lived in time and we're still wrapped in sound and movement – gull-glide, gull-swoop. We live time out, long bundles of bone bedded in the cliff.

I am the cliff. Keep away from me. I'm jumpy and shrinking, unsure of myself. I may let you down badly.

Layers and bands, boulders and gravel and grit and little shining stones: these are earth's bones. But the sea-god keeps laughing and crying and digging and tugging. I scarcely know where I am and I know time is ending. Fences. Red flags. Keep away from me. I'm not fit for the living.

We are the living. One night half of a cottage – Peter's cottage – bucketed down into the boiling water and he was left standing on the cliff-edge in his night-shirt.

After that, everyone wanted to move inland. We had no choice. You've only to look at the cracks. To listen to the sea-god's hollow voice!

Every year he comes closer. Gordon's cottage went down. And Martha's. And Ellen's. The back of the village

became the front. And now what's left? Only the
bellwoman's cottage, and the empty shell of the church.

I am the church. I remember the days when the
bellows wheezed for the organ to play. I remember
when people got down on their knees and prayed.

I've weathered such storms. Winds tearing at the
walls, flint-and-brick, salt winds howling.

And now, tonight, this storm. So fierce, old earth
herself is shaking and shuddering. Ah! Here comes the
old bellwoman.

I am the bellwoman. There! Those lights, stuttering and
bouncing. There's a boat out there, and maybe ten.

Up, up these saucer steps as fast as I can. Up!

Here in this mouldy room, I'll ring and ring and
ring, and set heaven itself singing, until my palms are
raw. I'll drown the sea-god.

I am the sea-god. And I keep clapping my luminous
hands.

Come this way, fisherman, over the seal's bath
and here along the cockle-path. Here are the slick
quicksands, and they will have you.

Fisherman, come this way over the gulls' road and
the herring-haunt! Here, up against this crumbling cliff.
Give me your boat.

I am the boat. To keep afloat; to go where my master tells me: I've always obeyed the two commandments.

Now my master says forward but the sea-god says back; my master says anchor but the night-storm says drag. My deck is a tangle of lines and nets and ropes; my old heart's heavy with sluicing dark water. I'm drowning; I'm torn apart.

Groan and creak: I quiver; I weep salt. Shouts of the fishermen. Laughter of the sea-god. Scream of the night-storm.

I am the night-storm. I AM THE STORM.

Down with the bell and down with the belfry. Down on the white head of the bellwoman. Down with the whole church and the tilting graveyard. Down with the cliff itself, cracking and opening and sliding and collapsing. Down with them all into the foam-and-snarl of the sea.

I'm the night-storm and there will be no morning.

I am the morning. I am good morning.

My hands are white as white doves, and healing. Let me lay them on this purple fever. Let them settle on the boat.

Nothing lasts for ever. Let me give you back your eyes, fisherman.

I am the fisherman. I heard the bell last night. Joe and Grimus and Pug, yes we all did! I heard the bell and dropped anchor. But there is no bell. There's no church, there's no belfry along this coast. Where am I? Am I dreaming?

Well! God blessed this old boat and our haul of shiners. He saw fit to spare us sinners. We'll take our bearings, now, and head for home.

But I heard the bell. And now! I can hear it! Down, down under the boat's keel. I can hear the bell.

I am the bell. I am the tongue of the bell, gold and green, far under the swinging water.

I ring and ring, in fog and storm, to save boats from the quicksands and the rocky shore. I'm like to last; I'm cast in bronze, I weigh two tons.

Listen now! Can you hear me? Can you hear the changes of the sea?

Kevin Crossley-Holland